GET INFORMED—STAY INFORMED

OIL AND PIPELINES

Natalie Hyde

CRABTREE
PUBLISHING COMPANY
WWW.CRABTREEBOOKS.COM

Author: Natalie Hyde
Series research and development: Reagan Miller
Editor-in-chief: Lionel Bender
Editor: Ellen Rodger
Proofreaders: Laura Booth, Melissa Boyce
Project coordinator: Petrice Custance
Design and photo research: Ben White
Production: Kim Richardson
Production coordinator and prepress technician: Tammy McGarr
Print coordinator: Katherine Berti
Consultant: Emily Drew, The New York Public Library

Produced for Crabtree Publishing Company by Bender Richardson White

Photographs and reproductions: Alamy: 6–7 (danilo pinzon, jr), 15 (Falkenstein/Bildagentur-online Historical Collect.), 16–17 (Lisa Werner), 20–21 (Design Pics Inc), 22–23 (Lloyd Sutton), 24–25 (Xinhua), 25 (Newscom), 28 (ZUMA Press, Inc.), 28–29 (America), 30–31 (Michael Wheatley Photography), 34 (UrbanImages), 39 (Nord Stream Ag/Russian Look/ZUMA Wire); Getty Images: 4–5 (Getty Images), 18–19 (Pacific Press), 32–33 (Brittany Sowacke/Bloomberg), 36–37 (Brent Lewin/Bloomberg), 37 (Shawn Thew/Bloomberg), 42–43 (NurPhoto); Shutterstock: 1 (NYCStock), 6 (Ulga), 7 (Melinda Fawver), 8–9 (Sergei Bachlakov), 10 top (rawpixel.com), 10 bottom (Alexander Oganezov), 10–11 (reisegraf.ch), 12–13 (Anton Foltin), 14–15 (MAGNIFIER), 26 (North Monaco), 26–27 (Brian Kinney), 33 (G B Hart), 34–35 (Alexander Oganezov), 38–39 (Igor Grochev), 40 (Erika J Mitchell), 40–41 (Oleksiy Mark), 43 (Monkey Business Images); Icons & heading band: shutterstock.com

Diagrams: Stefan Chabluk, using the following as sources of data: p. 13: U.S. Energy Information Association, University of Calgary/Energy Education, p.17: Canadian Energy Pipeline Association, p. 18: U.S. Census Bureau, NOAA, p. 22: U.S. Bureau of Labor Statistics, p. 28: Undark.org/Medium Corporation, p. 33: Oil and Gas Journal, p. 38: Statista.com.

Library and Archives Canada Cataloguing in Publication

Hyde, Natalie, 1963-, author
Oil and gas pipelines / Natalie Hyde.

(Get informed -- stay informed)
Includes bibliographical references and index.
Issued in print and electronic formats.
ISBN 978-0-7787-5334-6 (hardcover).--
ISBN 978-0-7787-5348-3 (softcover).--
ISBN 978-1-4271-2195-0 (HTML)

1. Petroleum pipelines--Political aspects--Juvenile literature. 2. Natural gas pipelines--Political aspects--Juvenile literature. 3. Petroleum pipelines--Environmental aspects--Juvenile literature. 4. Natural gas pipelines--Environmental aspects--Juvenile literature. 5. Petroleum industry and trade--Political aspects--Juvenile literature. 6. Gas industry--Political aspects--Juvenile literature. 7. Petroleum industry and trade--Environmental aspects--Juvenile literature. 8. Gas industry--Environmental aspects--Juvenile literature. I. Title.

TN879.5.H93 2019 j665.5'44 C2018-905652-5 C2018-905653-3

Library of Congress Cataloging-in-Publication Data

Names: Hyde, Natalie, 1963- author.
Title: Oil and pipelines / Natalie Hyde.
Description: New York : Crabtree Publishing Company, [2019] | Series: Get informed--stay informed | Includes bibliographical references and index.
Identifiers: LCCN 2018057992 (print) | LCCN 2019000356 (ebook) | ISBN 9781427121950 (Electronic) | ISBN 9780778753346 (hardcover : alk. paper) | ISBN 9780778753483 (pbk. : alk. paper)
Subjects: LCSH: Petroleum pipelines--Environmental aspects--United States--Juvenile literature. | Petroleum reserves--Environmental aspects--United States--Juvenile literature.
Classification: LCC TD195.P5 (ebook) | LCC TD195.P5 H93 2019 (print) | DDC 388.5/50973--dc23
LC record available at https://lccn.loc.gov/2018057992

Crabtree Publishing Company
www.crabtreebooks.com 1-800-387-7650

Printed in the U.S.A./032019/CG20190118

Published in Canada
Crabtree Publishing
616 Welland Ave.
St. Catharines, ON
L2M 5V6

Published in the United States
Crabtree Publishing
PMB 59051
350 Fifth Avenue, 59th Floor
New York, NY 10118

Published in the United Kingdom
Crabtree Publishing
Maritime House
Basin Road North, Hove
BN41 1WR

Published in Australia
Crabtree Publishing
Unit 3 – 5 Currumbin Court
Capalaba
QLD 4157

CONTENTS

1 PIPELINES CONTROVERSY

Toothbrushes, running shoes, cell phones, and lifesaving drugs are just some of the products made with natural oil and gas that we use in our daily lives. Travel, jobs, clothing, and electricity all depend on the **petrochemical** industry. While **renewable energies**, such as solar and wind power, are becoming more common, most of us still heat our water and homes and cook with oil and natural gas. These are transported across country by pipelines.

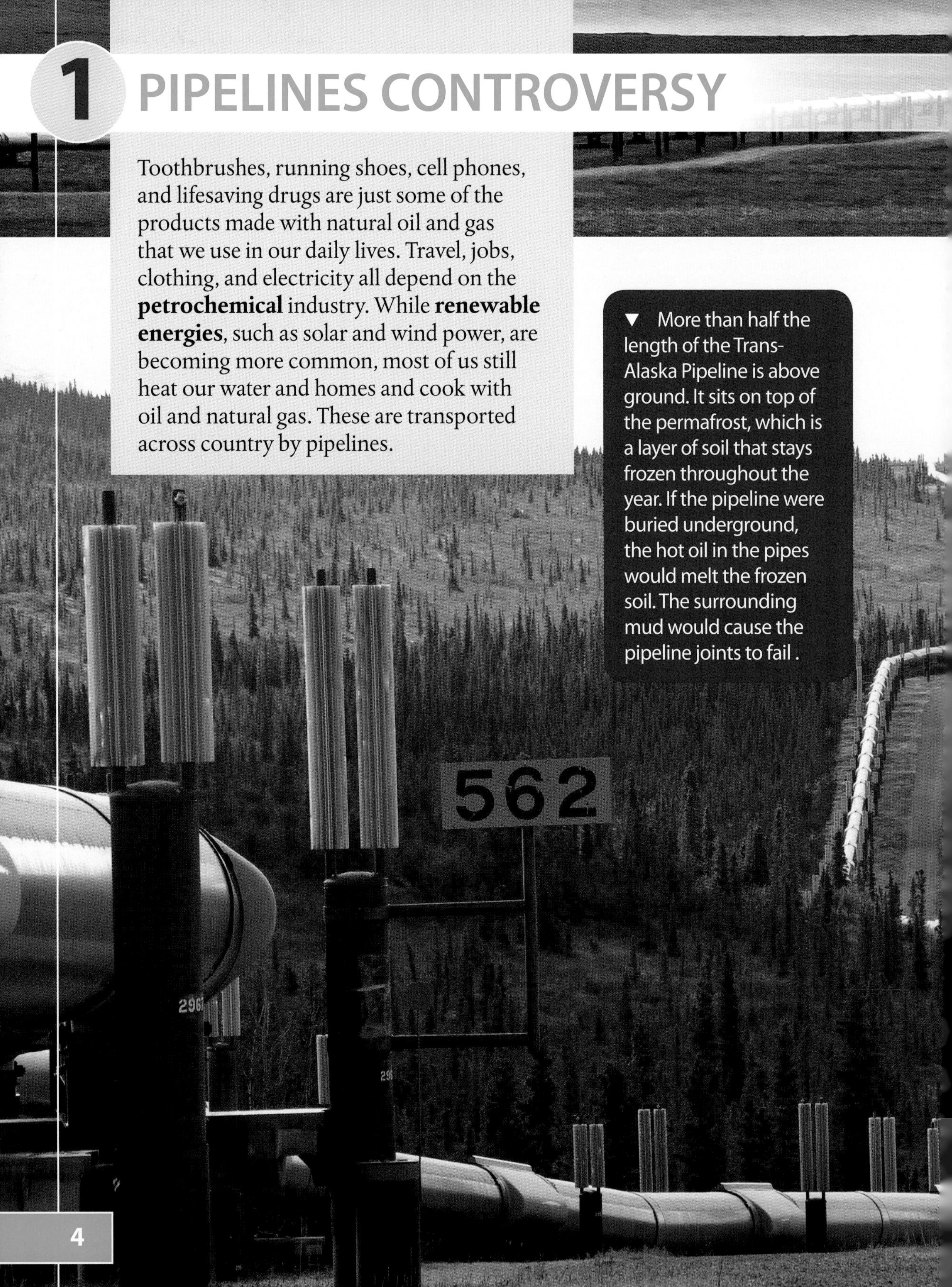

▼ More than half the length of the Trans-Alaska Pipeline is above ground. It sits on top of the permafrost, which is a layer of soil that stays frozen throughout the year. If the pipeline were buried underground, the hot oil in the pipes would melt the frozen soil. The surrounding mud would cause the pipeline joints to fail .

QUESTIONS TO ASK

Within this book are three types of boxes with questions to help your critical thinking about oil and gas pipelines. The icons will help you identify them.

THE CENTRAL ISSUES
Learning about the main points of information.

WHAT'S AT STAKE
Helping you determine how the issue will affect you.

ASK YOUR OWN QUESTIONS
Prompts to address gaps in your understanding.

POLLUTING CONTENTS

There are thousands of miles of pipelines that bring oil and gas to processing plants and into our homes. Pipelines are needed but they sometimes break or explode, and their contents pollutes the area around them. Building pipelines can destroy natural habitats and block animal migration routes. The oil and gas in the pipes are **fossil fuels**, which release the gas carbon dioxide (CO_2) when they are burned. This gas is a major contributor to climate change. If we continue to use oil and gas at our present rate, our planet may become unlivable.

FORMING AN OPINION

Because oil and gas and products made from them are found in every part of our lives, the building and care of pipelines that transport them is a topic that affects everyone. Knowing how the pipelines affect our **economy**, our environment, and our lifestyle is important when you begin to make decisions about how you want to live your life. Getting informed about a topic or issue is the first step in having an opinion about it and making your voice heard in the related discussion and **debate**.

> "*The pipeline debate is being framed as either/or. Either we cannot have pipelines or we cannot protect the environment .... We can have both, in that we can protect the environment ... allowing development to proceed in an orderly fashion.*"
>
> Jim Boucher, chief of Alberta's Fort McKay First Nation

PUTTING PIPELINES IN CONTEXT

It's easy to dismiss topics that seem too big or too complicated to figure out. It can be scary to learn about things threatening our health and our world. But some topics, such as the **controversy** over oil and gas pipelines, are important to understand. The direction we move in as a **society** will have consequences for everyone.

The **key** players in this issue have their own reasons for wanting you to agree with their side. **Politicians** who decide if pipelines are built want to be re-elected. Oil and gas companies want to continue to make a profit. Environmentalists and farmers want to protect our natural world. Communities want to make sure everyone can find cheap, reliable fuel and products for everyday living. Governments want to make sure there are jobs.

SETTING THE SCENE

For any topic, the context—the setting or framework around it—plays a part. The context for oil and gas pipelines is a

▶ Natural gas is piped into many homes. Stoves using natural gas cost about half as much to run as electric stoves. They also can be used during power outages, unlike electric stoves. However, some people worry about possible gas leaks.

▶ Plastics of many types used in these children's toys, for example, are made from **crude oil** and natural gas. The oil and gas are refined, or treated, in special ways, then mixed with other materials.

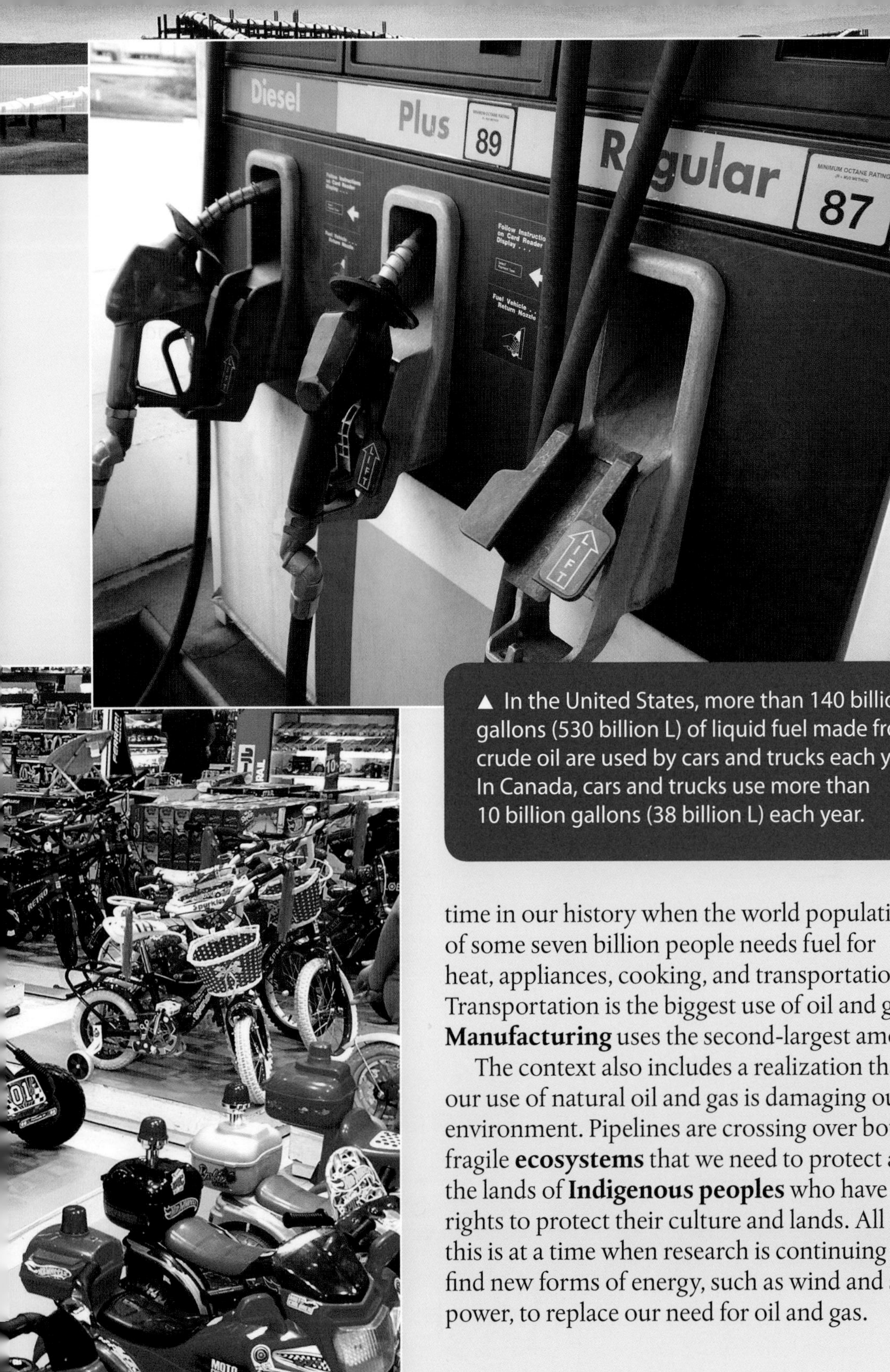

▲ In the United States, more than 140 billion gallons (530 billion L) of liquid fuel made from crude oil are used by cars and trucks each year. In Canada, cars and trucks use more than 10 billion gallons (38 billion L) each year.

time in our history when the world population of some seven billion people needs fuel for heat, appliances, cooking, and transportation. Transportation is the biggest use of oil and gas. **Manufacturing** uses the second-largest amount.

The context also includes a realization that our use of natural oil and gas is damaging our environment. Pipelines are crossing over both fragile **ecosystems** that we need to protect and the lands of **Indigenous peoples** who have rights to protect their culture and lands. All of this is at a time when research is continuing to find new forms of energy, such as wind and solar power, to replace our need for oil and gas.

2 HOW TO GET INFORMED

So, where do you begin to get informed about a topic? It is always useful to dig into the history of the topic. Look for answers to why and how the controversy began. Who are the key players in the debate? What are the main issues? What are the special terms and concepts that you should know? When looking at oil and gas pipelines you will come across terms such as **fracking**, crude oil, **refineries**, and migration routes. Understanding the meaning and importance of these will help you see the full picture.

KEY PLAYERS

Oil and gas pipeline companies, such as Kinder Morgan, Enbridge, and the Williams Companies, make their money building and maintaining pipelines. Kinder Morgan operates about 85,000 miles (136,800 km) of pipeline. Enbridge works in both Canada and the United States and has the longest transportation system in North America. The Williams Companies, based in Oklahoma in the United States, mainly deals with processing and transporting natural gas.

DIFFERENT VIEWPOINTS

You will quickly notice that information from each key player will have a different slant or emphasis. Each person or group involved in the topic has their own opinions and beliefs. Companies providing oil and gas through pipelines will see the number of leaks or breaks one way—perhaps just as accidents. Environmentalists who document the effects on groundwater and wildlife will see it differently—as disasters. These differences become clear when anything, from a report to a photograph, is created. This is called bias. To become well informed, you have to first recognize that there is bias. Almost all information contains some level of bias. By recognizing it and allowing for it in your thoughts, you will get a balanced view of the topic.

TIME AND PLACE

Judging whether information is accurate or reliable can be tricky. Historians use the Time and Place Rule to help them. This rule states that the closer to an event or person that material is created, the more likely it is to be reliable. A report on the damage to the environment due to a pipeline rupturing will be more accurate if it is written within days of the event rather than an article written based on people's memories a year later. So when forming an opinion on a topic, choice of material is very important.

◀ In April 2012, thousands of people in Vancouver, Canada, took part in an Earth Day Parade where they protested the building of a second Kinder Morgan Trans Mountain Pipeline to carry crude oil from Edmonton, Alberta, to Burnaby, British Columbia.

▲ When researching a topic, libraries are a good source of both print and digital material.

KEY INFORMATION

Primary sources are firsthand evidence of a topic, made by the people involved in or who witnessed the events. An image of a pipeline protest is one example. **Secondary sources** are reports, analyses, and **interpretations** of the primary sources, such as government statistics on the number of pipeline leaks in a given time period. **Tertiary sources** are summaries or **databases** of primary and secondary information. They include things such as Wikipedia articles or entries in encyclopedias.

NOTICE:
WARNING
PETROLEUM
PIPELINE
BEFORE EXCAVATING OR IN EMERGENCY
PLEASE CALL
OLYMPIC PIPE LINE CO.
(888) 271-8880
WARNING

▲ Warning signs help prevent construction equipment, road-repair workmen, or farmers' tractors from accidentally hitting buried pipelines.

▶ Aboveground pipelines like this one affect the habits of wildlife by interfering with hunting territories and the migration, or natural movement, of large animals.

> *We cannot allow polluting corporations to lock us into decades of dependence on fracked gas when clean, renewable energy sources are affordable and abundant right now.*
>
> Michael Brune, Sierra Club Executive Director

Everything created about a topic is called source material. Source material can be written—for example, newspaper articles and magazine reports. It can be visual items such as photographs, diagrams, or maps. It can be oral, including recorded interviews or songs. Source material can also include artifacts, or made objects, such as coins, tools, or pottery. Studying and **analyzing** source material is how we learn what, why, and how something has happened.

Where should you look for source material? Museums, libraries, exhibits, and monuments can be sources of historical information. For more current events or topics, newspapers and magazines will have articles you can research. The Internet has plenty of resources. Online news sites will have up-to-date stories and facts. Some are geared to delivering the news to youth—they include *TIME for Kids, TweenTribune,* and *The Washington Post KidsPost*. You can also find source material on blogs, **social media** sites, and podcasts. Government reports, research papers, and **statistics** also provide information. Maps of where pipelines are located can give you an idea of how many places are affected by them.

SPECIFIC INFORMATION

Look for source material with different viewpoints. For oil and gas pipelines, you can research source material from:

- energy and transportation companies' reports
- environmental groups' websites
- interviews with Indigenous peoples
- governments' statistics and laws.

All these key players have different **agendas** and concerns. Remembering this will help you get a balanced view of the issue.

Every topic has its own unique terms, vocabulary, and ideas. The oil and gas industry has **specialized** machinery, processes, and products. To evaluate the information you will be reading, you will need a good understanding of everything in your source material. It's not always best to just ask friends and family what something means. Even definitions can carry bias or can be slanted by the opinions and beliefs of others. It is a good idea to start with a dictionary or glossary, either in print or online, for a basic definition. These are created to be unbiased.

DEFINITIONS AND STATISTICS

Terms and ideas you might encounter while researching oil and gas pipelines could include nonrenewable energy, climate change, Indigenous rights, and endangered species. Be aware that explanations of some ideas or terms may reflect the beliefs or agenda of the person or group supplying it. The idea of **land claims** might be described to you by a large energy company as a costly delay in expanding a business. To the Indigenous community, land claims are a battle for respect, an upholding of **treaties**, and the protection of their

▶ This fracking equipment is blasting a **pressurized** mixture of water, sand, and chemicals into the ground to create cracks in the rocks deep underground to release the oil or natural gas. These products are then transported by pipelines to the nationwide network or grid.

MAP OF NORTH AMERICA SHOWING MAJOR OIL AND GAS PIPELINES

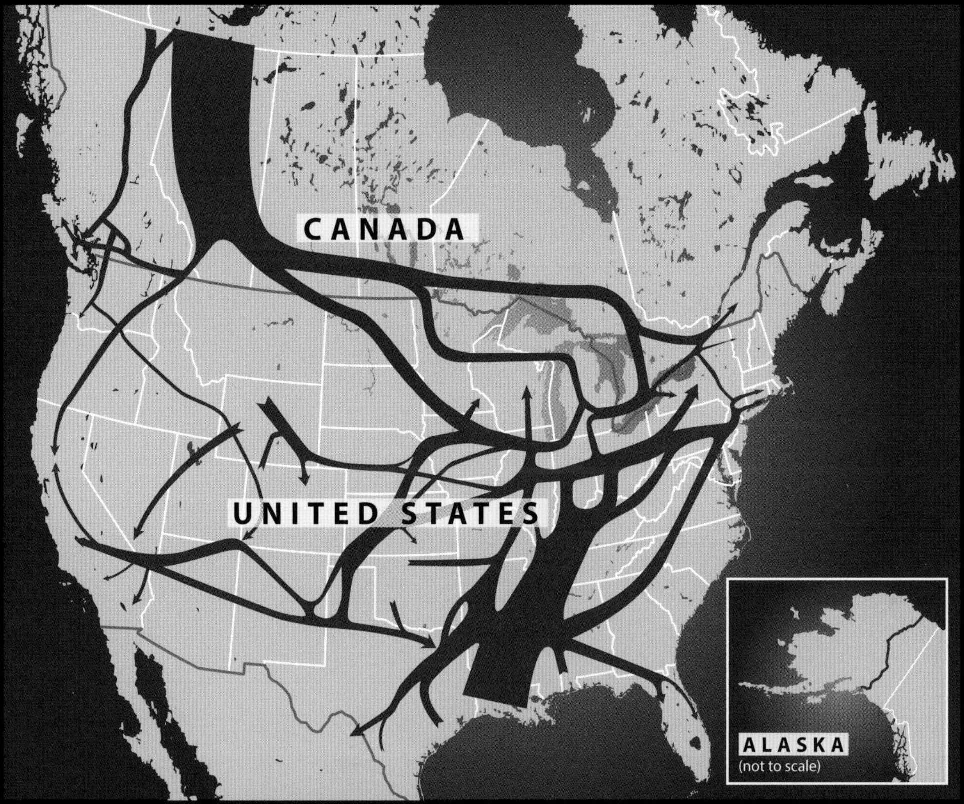

CANADA

UNITED STATES

ALASKA
(not to scale)

The thicker the route, the greater the volume of oil and gas distributed.

culture, **community**, and history. If you are unsure if a term has a biased definition, try to look at two **opposing** groups for the meanings they give. The **objective** definition is usually found somewhere between those two.

Graphics and statistics can give a lot of information in a small amount of space. But even they can show bias. Charts, graphs, pie charts, and tables just present data, but it is up to you to draw conclusions from them. It is important to recognize any bias so your conclusions are accurate. A government chart might show that more pipelines mean more jobs. An environmental group might show the same number of pipelines, but relate it to the amount of destruction to ecosystems.

3 HOW DID WE GET HERE?

Pipelines have been used to transport oil and gas since the 1800s. Some train engines used oil as fuel, and natural gas was used to provide lighting in cities starting in 1816. When cars were invented in the early 1900s, the need for oil increased. Central heating in houses and buildings created a demand for oil in furnaces. As oil and gas heating began to replace coal and wood to heat homes and buildings, the demand for these fuels increased. Pipelines became the best way to bring these products to consumers.

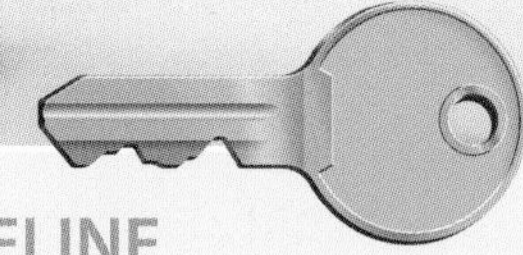

TIMELINE

Key oil and gas pipelines in North America

1853 First pipeline in Canada moves natural gas about 16 miles (25.7 km) to Trois Rivières, Quebec.

1859 First pipeline in the United States brings natural gas from a well to the town of Titusville, Pennsylvania.

1953 Trans Mountain Pipeline begins shipping oil from Edmonton, Alberta, to Burnaby, British Columbia.

1985 The biggest spill of the Trans Mountain Pipeline spills about 10,000 barrels of oil near Edmonton.

2012 Kinder Morgan announces plans to expand the Trans Mountain Pipeline.

January 2016 Plans are approved for the Dakota Access Pipeline.

August 2016 Members of the Standing Rock Sioux Tribe block the construction site.

March 2017 The U.S. judge denies the injunction of local Sioux and Cheyenne tribes. Construction begins again.

2018 The federal government of Canada decides to buy the Trans Mountain Pipeline after Kinder Morgan decides to suspend the expansion project.

◀ Pipelines bring crude oil into refineries like this one. Then it is refined into everyday products we use such as gasoline, kerosene, and jet fuel.

EARLY USE OF PIPELINES

The first pipelines were made of wood or clay. Clay pipes were strong but could collapse under high pressure. Tree roots could work their way into joints and cause them to break apart. Today, oil and natural gas are transported in steel or plastic pipes. The pipes are usually buried several feet under the ground. Sometimes they are coated in concrete or covered in sand underground to prevent the pipelines weakening from ice, extreme temperatures, or pressure.

As more oil and gas was needed, pipelines replaced wagons and railroads for transporting fossil fuels. It was a cheaper and faster way to move them. Pipelines could reduce transportation costs by half. The first oil and gas pipelines in North America were short. They took oil from drill holes to storage tanks or refineries. As pipelines were made bigger, longer, and in more complicated networks, the dangers to people and the environment also became a bigger problem.

REGISTERED

REGISTERED

25000

NUMBER RU 1096

MICHIGAN WISCONSIN PIPE LINE COMPANY

FIRST MORTGAGE PIPE LINE BOND, 9⅝% SERIES DUE 1994

RU 1096 C000008 L F ROTHSCHILD & CO

9⅝% DUE 1994

TWENTY FIVE THOUSAND

CUSIP 594763 AP 9

DOLLARS

DATED JUN 12 1974

TRUSTEE'S CERTIFICATE

FIRST NATIONAL CITY BANK, AS TRUSTEE

▼ A historic stock certificate for buying shares in a pipeline company. Most pipeline companies are privately owned.

THE CENTRAL ISSUES

What are the dangers, both physical and environmental, to transporting oil and gas by pipelines? Is there an alternative to pipelines or will we always have this issue?

CONSTRUCTING A PIPELINE

Building a pipeline often involves several levels of government, from local to state or provincial to national, for applications and approvals. Pipelines cross all landforms. This means digging into stony or swampy ground or building aboveground supports. They can cause controversies. Environmentalists want to protect ecosystems and the water supply. Indigenous peoples want to protect and maintain control over their lands, which could be threatened by pollution and damage to their burial grounds.

RISKY BUSINESS

Even after pipelines are built, they are still a threat to safety and the environment. Many things can damage pipes. The steel or iron can become weaker with age. It can begin to leak or be damaged by erosion from rocks or ice. Natural disasters, such as earthquakes or tornadoes, can cause pipelines to break.

The oil or gas flowing through pipelines is pressurized. If the pipe ruptures or cracks, the fuel inside will burst out. This will cause an explosion. If there is a spark, it can catch fire. Pipeline explosions cause **toxic** spills, injuries, and even deaths. The worst pipeline accident in Canadian history was the LaSalle Heights Disaster in Lasalle, Quebec, in 1965. The gas line explosion killed 28 people, injured 39, and left 200 homeless. That same year, there was also a pipeline failure in the United States, in Louisiana. Seventeen people died when that pipeline exploded.

While recent pipeline failures have not resulted in as many deaths and injuries, these past events remind the public of the risks. Most steel pipes have a lifespan of 20 to 50 years. If they are left too long, the pipes will leak or burst. Eventually they become weak and need to be replaced. That costs a lot of money and means digging up and disturbing the ground again.

KEY PLAYERS

The **Canadian Energy Pipeline Association** (CEPA) represents pipeline companies. The members of this organization transport 97 percent of the oil and natural gas produced in Canada. CEPA works to improve pipeline safety and is proud that Canada's pipeline industry has a high safety record. It also helps companies work with Indigenous communities and landowners.

▶ An oil leak at Refugio State Beach in California in 2015 led to a protest over an oil pipeline along the coastline. Oil cleanups are difficult and expensive and kill large numbers of fish and sea birds. Since 1986, there have been more than 8,000 pipeline **incidents** in the United States.

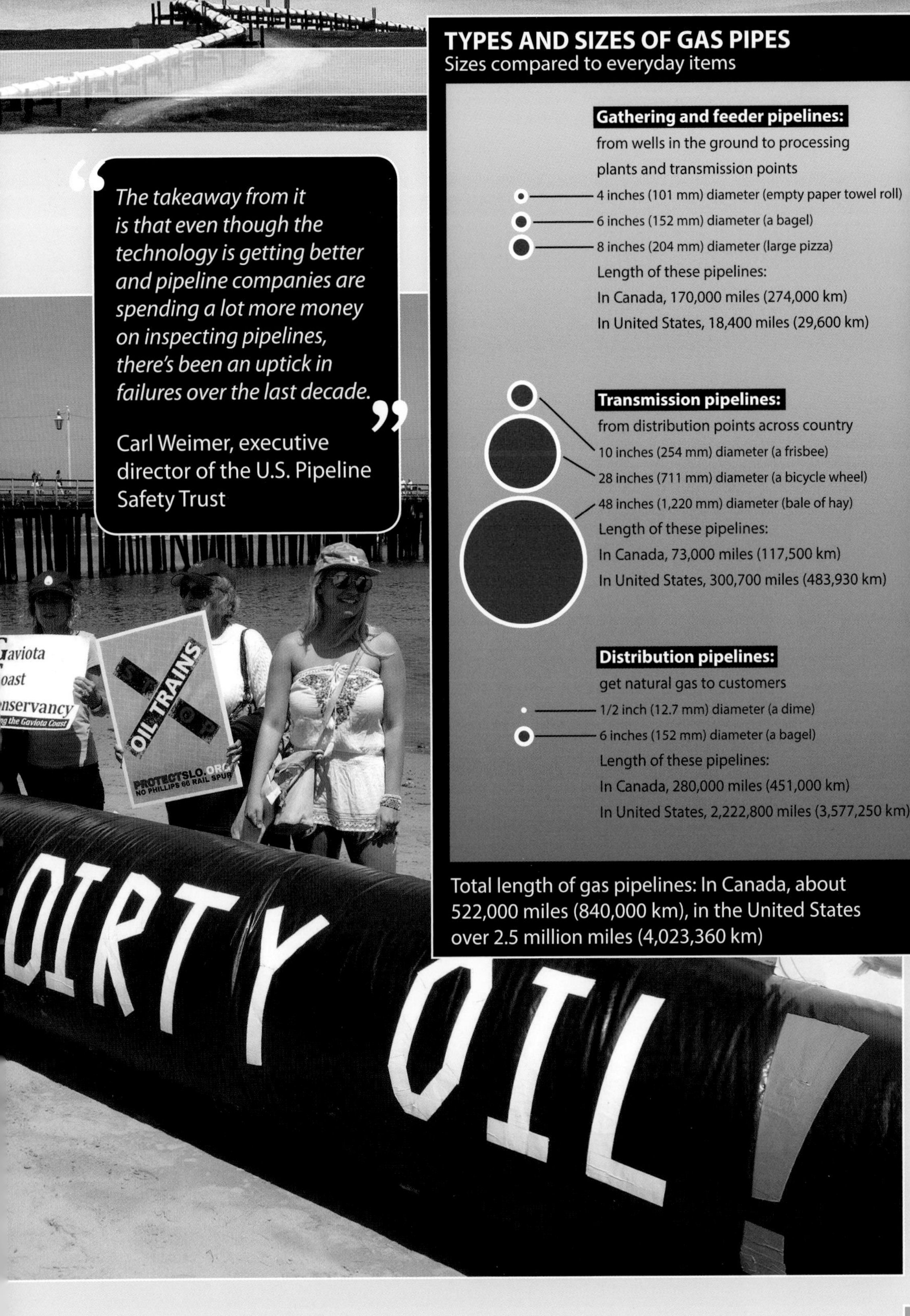

"The takeaway from it is that even though the technology is getting better and pipeline companies are spending a lot more money on inspecting pipelines, there's been an uptick in failures over the last decade."

Carl Weimer, executive director of the U.S. Pipeline Safety Trust

TYPES AND SIZES OF GAS PIPES

Sizes compared to everyday items

Gathering and feeder pipelines:

from wells in the ground to processing plants and transmission points

4 inches (101 mm) diameter (empty paper towel roll)

6 inches (152 mm) diameter (a bagel)

8 inches (204 mm) diameter (large pizza)

Length of these pipelines:

In Canada, 170,000 miles (274,000 km)

In United States, 18,400 miles (29,600 km)

Transmission pipelines:

from distribution points across country

10 inches (254 mm) diameter (a frisbee)

28 inches (711 mm) diameter (a bicycle wheel)

48 inches (1,220 mm) diameter (bale of hay)

Length of these pipelines:

In Canada, 73,000 miles (117,500 km)

In United States, 300,700 miles (483,930 km)

Distribution pipelines:

get natural gas to customers

1/2 inch (12.7 mm) diameter (a dime)

6 inches (152 mm) diameter (a bagel)

Length of these pipelines:

In Canada, 280,000 miles (451,000 km)

In United States, 2,222,800 miles (3,577,250 km)

Total length of gas pipelines: In Canada, about 522,000 miles (840,000 km), in the United States over 2.5 million miles (4,023,360 km)

▶ In December 2016, protesters of the Dakota Access Pipeline gathered at Oceti Sakowin Camp on Indigenous land and then marched in driving snow toward a barricade on Highway 1806. The protest had already been going on for more than a year.

INDIGENOUS LANDS

Indigenous peoples have always been especially connected to the environment. The health of the land and water is very important to their culture, lifestyle, and traditions. Over time, certain sites came to hold special meaning for them, either as a place of burial, or a place where ceremonies were held. The location of these sites and their importance was passed down from generation to generation.

KEY PLAYERS

The Association of Oil Pipe Lines (AOPL) was established in 1947 and represents owners and operators of pipelines in the United States. This organization **lobbies** for laws that protect their industry and their workers. They are also a place that the government can contact in case of natural disasters affecting pipelines.

VITAL LIFE-FORCE

To build a pipeline, ground has to be dug up and disrupted for hundreds of miles. This can affect areas that have spiritual meaning for Indigenous peoples. Some of these sites have an ancient history that is known to Indigenous peoples but has left no visible signs. And it isn't just building the pipeline that disturbs the land. After they are built, leaks and explosions release **toxins** into the ground. The land isn't the only thing polluted by pipeline failures—so is water. Water is a vital life-force for all living things. Human-made structures that damage the environment are in direct conflict with Indigenous peoples' belief in caring for the Earth.

Many Indigenous groups still follow hunting and fishing methods used by their ancestors. Underground pipeline failures can affect the land's ability to supply them with healthy plants and animals. Leaks into rivers, lakes, and oceans can kill fish and **marine** plants and animals. Aboveground pipelines limit some migration routes or territories, throwing the number and variety of the animals living nearby out of balance. These situations have a direct result on the living conditions of Indigenous peoples relying on the land and water for food.

4 INFORMATION LITERACY

The topic of oil and gas pipelines is constantly changing. We are using more oil, gas, and **petroleum products** than ever before. New pipelines are still being planned and built. They are also still breaking, exploding, and leaking, as many age or are damaged in natural disasters. You need to develop a strategy to follow the changes.

▶ This oil refinery in the oil sands of Alberta, Canada, shows the damage to the surrounding area, with deforested land, piles of overturned earth, and pipelines bringing in crude oil.

> *The fact is, this country needs to end its addiction to oil.*
>
> Frances Beinecke, former president of the U.S. Natural Resources Defense Council

KEEPING AN OPEN MIND

Studying a range of relevant source materials and then sorting and evaluating the information they contain is known as information literacy. It is a key part of getting informed. But as you search through articles, podcasts, and news programs, be aware of misinformation. Every group, industry, corporation, and government slants information to support its message. Sometimes people choose to believe what they read or hear because it fits with what they already think about a topic. Anything that might not agree with that idea is dismissed as false.

Just because an opinion is popular doesn't necessarily mean it's true. Every fact should be checked with experts or objective sources. It is not always easy to speak your concerns or to question. It can be uncomfortable to disagree with family and friends. But asking questions is how you get to the truth about something. Keeping an open mind by looking at the issue of oil and gas pipelines from different **perspectives** will help you find a balanced view.

WHAT'S AT STAKE?

What items or services made with petroleum products would you be willing to give up or change in your life in order to reduce your country's dependency on oil and gas?

GOVERNMENT PERSPECTIVE

The viewpoint of the government is that it is responsible for the country's needs. It must keep residents supplied with energy and products to improve their lives. It needs to create jobs. Selling fossil fuels to other countries is important to the nation's **economy**. The government sees pipelines as necessary to transport fuel from their source across borders or to ports.

EFFECTS ON COMMUNITIES

Every community depends on fuel for heating, cooking, and transportation. Keeping fuel prices low means everyone has money left over for other bills. Easy access to fuel means people don't struggle to stay warm or get to jobs. By simply turning on a hot water tap or using a pump at a gas station, everyone can enjoy the benefits of oil and gas.

Many communities rely on the oil and gas industry for jobs. More than one million people in the United States and 500,000 in Canada work in oil- and gas-related jobs. Building, running, and repairing pipelines is important to the economy of many towns. But this **dependence** on fossil fuels comes at a price. The industry can cause noise and light pollution for the people living nearby. Trucks and machinery damage roads and increase traffic.

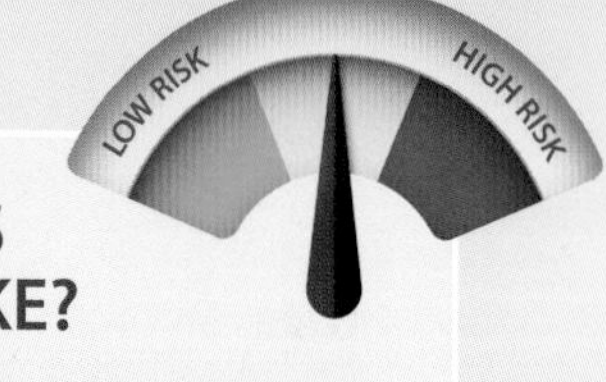

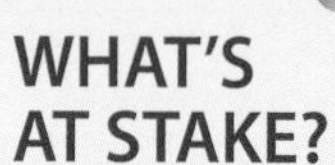
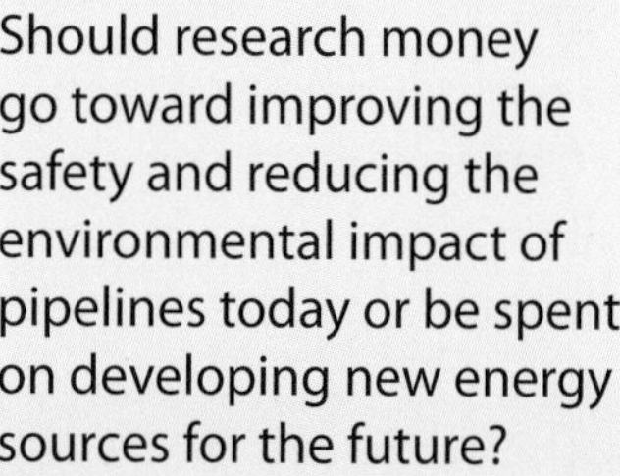

WHAT'S AT STAKE?

Should research money go toward improving the safety and reducing the environmental impact of pipelines today or be spent on developing new energy sources for the future?

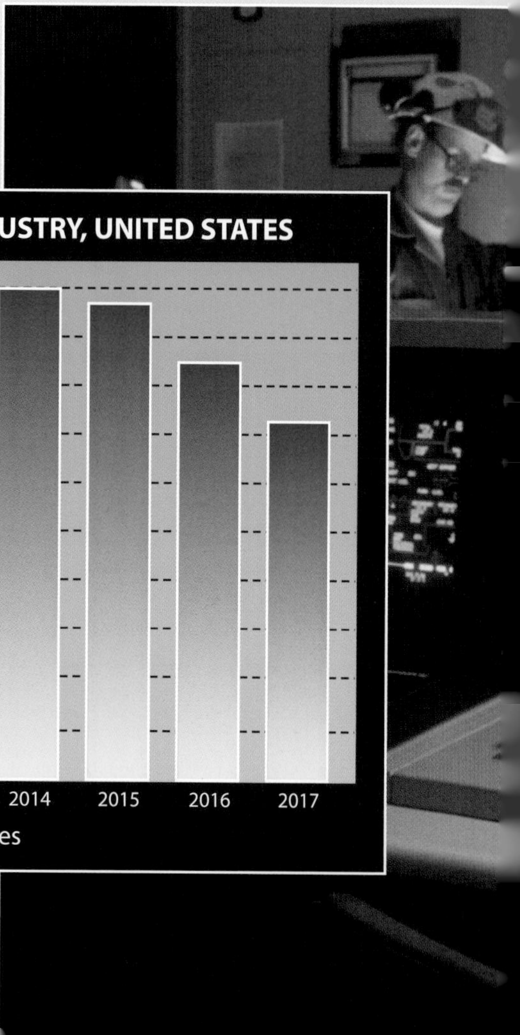

EMPLOYMENT IN THE OIL AND GAS PIPELINE INDUSTRY, UNITED STATES

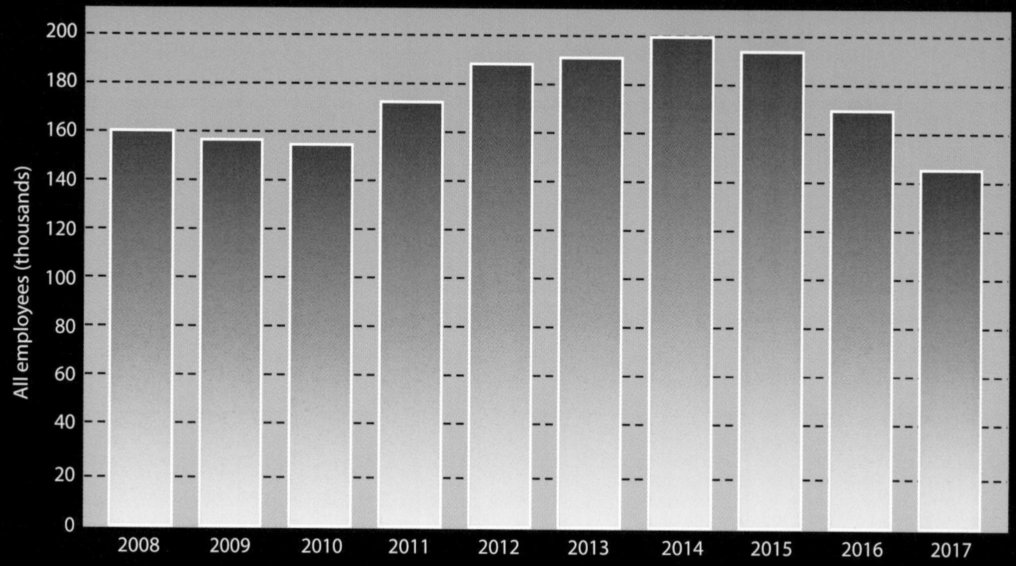

All employees (thousands)

200
180
160
140
120
100
80
60
40
20
0

2008 2009 2010 2011 2012 2013 2014 2015 2016 2017

Includes drilling, distribution (pipelines), and support services

INJURIES AND ACCIDENTS

One of the biggest concerns for communities is pipeline accidents. In the United States, there have been almost 9,000 serious incidents in the last 30 years. In Canada, about 1,500 accidents in the last 20 years have caused damage, injuries, and even deaths. Besides the devastation to a family when a member is hurt or killed, it takes a toll on hospital and medical services. Pipeline fires, explosions, and spills can cause oil to **impact** the soil and air where adults work and children play. People may then breathe **contaminated** air, eat contaminated food from their garden, or even drink contaminated water.

> *"When an oil company executive tells American families that we don't need to be concerned with tar sands pipeline safety, it's not only misleading, it's insulting."*
>
> Tom Steyer, founder of NextGen America, an environmental **action group**

◀ Pipeline companies use cameras and sensors to monitor their pipelines for leaks. Equipment can detect problems and send crews to fix them within minutes.

The oil and gas pipeline issue has united some Indigenous groups and divided others. The Dakota Access Pipeline (DAPL) in the United States was one project that brought several Indigenous groups together. It drew attention to the concerns all Indigenous peoples have over pipelines crossing land of historical and cultural importance to them.

STAND WITH STANDING ROCK

The DAPL project was created to bring crude oil from North Dakota to a storage area in Illinois. Its 1,172-mile-long (1,886 km) planned route would pass under the Missouri River only half a mile from the Standing Rock Indian Reservation. A spill would have serious effects on the water supply for the Sioux people who live there.

Protests started in 2016 as soon as construction began. The Sioux demanded that the U.S. government do a study on the impact to the environment and their water supply. They founded three camps on the construction site, including the Sacred Stone Camp. The Standing Rock Sioux also turned to the **media** to gain public support. Many people from different walks of life joined to "Stand With Standing Rock." Despite the protests, the pipeline was completed. However, the protesters brought different Indigenous nations together to voice their general concerns over pipelines, spills, and the importance of their heritage.

FOR PIPELINES

In Canada, **First Nations** such as the Cree of Frog Lake, Alberta, have agreed to pipelines on or near their territories. The Cree own the Frog Lake Energy Resources Corporation. They feel that as long as the environment is protected, pipelines are welcome because they provide jobs and money for the band.

In the United States, the Southern Ute tribe in Colorado agreed to allow the oil and gas industry on their lands because it brought in much-needed money. Its company, the Red Willow Production Company, has expanded and made the Southern Ute very wealthy.

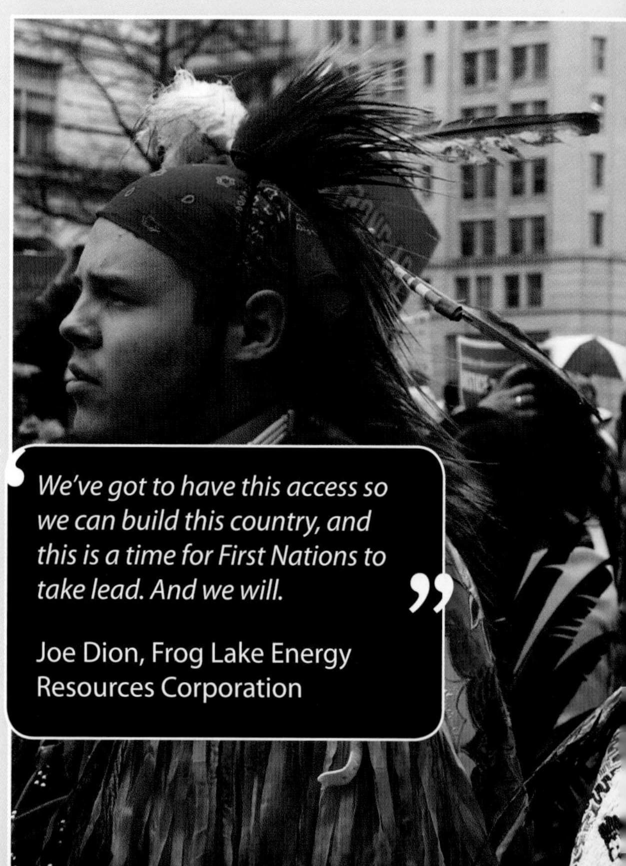

> *"We've got to have this access so we can build this country, and this is a time for First Nations to take lead. And we will."*
>
> Joe Dion, Frog Lake Energy Resources Corporation

KEY PLAYERS

Anti-pipeline groups, such as Climate Justice Edmonton, Greenpeace, and the Sierra Club, help organize protests and rallies. They are concerned about the pollution caused by the building and running of pipelines, as well as from spills, fires, and explosions.

▶ In June 2017, tribal leaders, including Southern Ute councilman Kevin Frost (second from left), met with President Donald Trump and government officials to discuss a balanced approach to using and managing tribal resources.

◀ Indigenous pipeline protesters at a rally in Washington, D.C., in March 2017, call on President Trump to respect their culture and honor their treaties.

▲ Using electric vehicles is one way of reducing the need for crude oil as a fuel, although fossil fuels are often used to generate electricity.

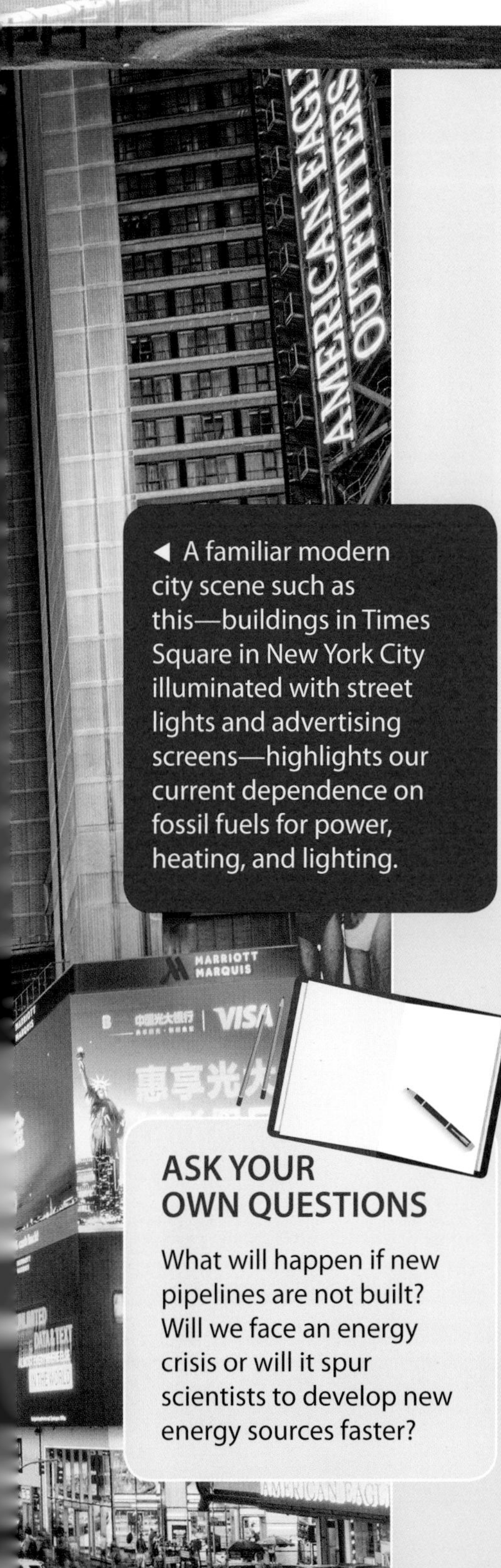

◀ A familiar modern city scene such as this—buildings in Times Square in New York City illuminated with street lights and advertising screens—highlights our current dependence on fossil fuels for power, heating, and lighting.

Oil and oil products are so valuable to the economy that people call it "black gold." As oil production and usage around the world constantly changes, so does the price of crude oil. This affects the economy of whole nations and is sometimes the cause of international strife. Natural gas is an economic item in similar ways.

MANUFACTURING NEEDS

The oil and gas industry is a major employer in the United States and Canada (see page 22) but the fossil fuels themselves play a vital role in other parts of the economy. Pipelines bring fuel for energy to almost all types of manufacturing.

Vehicle, clothing, food, steel, and other factories all need energy to run. Oil products run machines and tractors. Oil also is the fuel for transport trucks that bring items to market. When energy is cheap and **dependable**, costs can be kept low. Products and services are then less expensive for customers. If the price of oil and gas doubled, the price of manufactured goods would rise steeply.

WANTING SOMETHING NEW

New technology and inventions are pursued to improve lives. Pipelines have proved to be comparatively cheap, efficient, and reliable. The downside to having readily available fossil fuels delivered right to our homes or businesses is that new technology is developed more slowly. Solar and wind power, electric cars, and **biofuels** are being perfected. Many people believe, however, that new discoveries would be made faster if we needed new sources of energy more urgently. Instead of investing in more fossil fuel pipelines, environmental groups want the money invested in renewable energy.

ASK YOUR OWN QUESTIONS

What will happen if new pipelines are not built? Will we face an energy crisis or will it spur scientists to develop new energy sources faster?

EFFECTS ON THE ENVIRONMENT

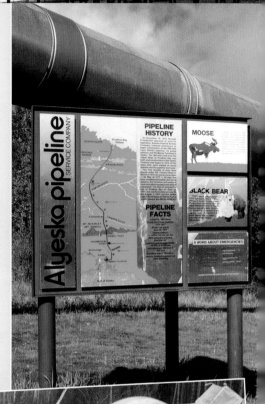

Pipelines are not built in straight lines. Planners avoid slopes or **fault lines** because they can cause cracks and leaks in the pipes. It is also expensive to blast or drill through rocky areas. Pipeline companies try to avoid areas with endangered wildlife. The planning process can take months to complete all the surveys. Pipeline companies also need to get permission and pay **compensation** to landowners along the route. Even with plans to avoid certain sensitive areas and damage to the environment, the pipeline route is one of the main reasons for oil and gas pipeline protests.

LAND AND WATER

When installing the pipes, the ground, forests, and waterways are disturbed. This changes the territory, food, and water for local animals. Their regular food and water sources could disappear. The stress could push endangered species to extinction.

▼ In June 2010, a pipeline leaked close to one million gallons of crude oil into the Kalamazoo River near Marshall, Michigan. It was one of the largest inland oil spills in American history. Turtles, ducks, and Canada geese had to be rescued and cleaned in order for them to survive.

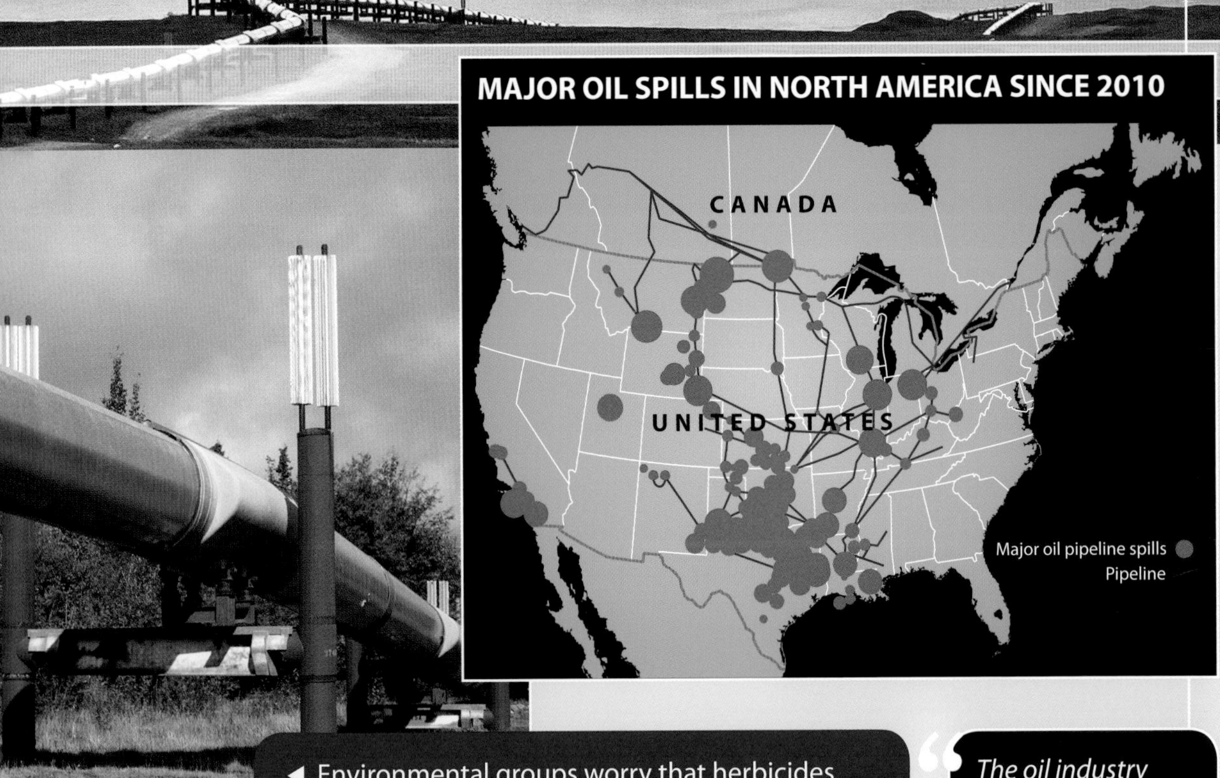

◄ Environmental groups worry that herbicides used to keep down weeds around pipelines could not only seep down into underground water sources, but also into lakes, ponds, and **wetlands**, affecting tree habitats, nests, or mineral licks.

> *"The oil industry says this is the safer way, but that doesn't mean this is safe. Property is damaged. People are killed. There is no way to safely transport fossil fuels."*
>
> Richard Stover, environmental advocate

The land itself is changed by the construction of oil and gas pipelines. The **fossil record** in the ground is disturbed. Trees are cut down, soil is moved, and plants are dug up. This can lead to erosion from wind and water or even landslides. Streams, rivers, and swamps can be affected. This can change water flow and drainage patterns. Every change in the environment has consequences to living things in the area, including humans.

Pollution is another big concern during the building and running of pipelines. Old-growth forests may be cut down on the route. Losing forests can contribute to climate change. Machinery from heavy equipment contributes to air pollution. Weed-killing chemicals to keep vegetation down around the pipes can seep into the ground. Spills and leaks can deposit **heavy metals**. These toxins can end up in the water supply, killing fish and making humans sick.

5 RECENT DEVELOPMENTS

Today, the United States energy pipelines travel more than 2.5 million miles (4 million km) around the country. Canadians get their oil and gas through more than 522,000 miles (840,000 km) of pipelines nationwide. With more people and businesses looking for good, cheap sources of oil and gas, energy companies are planning to expand.

▶ Protesters against the Trans Mountain Pipeline carry signs showing seals and fish. They want to remind people of the marine life that will be affected by spills from existing and new pipelines.

KEY PLAYERS

Indigenous groups, such as the Standing Rock Sioux Tribe, the Coast Salish peoples, and the Indigenous Environmental Network, are putting a lot of pressure on governments and energy companies. They see pipelines running through Indigenous lands as a symptom of a bigger problem of broken promises, ignored treaties, and **discrimination**. Some non-Indigenous people support them in their fight.

THE CENTRAL ISSUES

How can governments and businesses provide energy for customers but still respect Indigenous lands, culture, and traditions?

TRANS MOUNTAIN PIPELINE

New pipeline construction is facing a lot of debate and protest. Environmental groups are against more pipelines because it means more fossil fuel is being used. They are concerned that the increase will speed up climate change.

The Kinder Morgan Trans Mountain Expansion is a plan to add another pipeline alongside the existing Trans Mountain Pipeline from Alberta to the coast of British Columbia. This will mean double the amount of fossil fuel will be transported to markets around the world. It was opposed by several First Nations groups, environmental groups, and even the cities of Burnaby and Vancouver, B.C. In the end, the federal government of Canada stepped in and bought the pipeline so its construction could go ahead. This caused a lot of friction with Canadians who felt the government wasn't listening to their concerns.

KEYSTONE XL

Other projects are facing similar problems. The Keystone XL project is a plan to build a new pipeline from Alberta, Canada, to Nebraska in the U.S. It would travel through a fragile ecosystem in Sand Hills, Nebraska. It is an area of wetlands on the route for migrating birds. With water so near the surface, any spills or leaks would go directly into the ground water. The U.S. government under President Obama denied approval for it to go ahead. With a new government in control and new contracts for oil, construction for the pipeline may go ahead in 2019.

The Permian Basin is part of the oilfield in western Texas and southeastern New Mexico. More than 2.5 million barrels of oil are produced here every day. There are billions more barrels of oil and supplies of natural gas in the ground. About 1 million barrels per day (bpd) are shipped to other countries. If output increases, the United States could be the third-largest producer in the world.

ASK YOUR OWN QUESTIONS

Do you think oil and gas production will increase in the future or be replaced by renewable energy sources such as solar or wind power? Why? What facts or statistics back up your answer?

WHY MORE PIPELINES?

What would be the effect of twice as much oil and natural gas being pumped, shipped, and sold? The government knows that would be great for the economy, but what about the environment? Right now there is a **bottleneck** because the companies drilling for oil and gas cannot get the product to customers. To increase flow, new pipelines need to be built. This will be great in terms of jobs in the region, but it would also increase pollution.

Environmental groups are challenging oil and gas companies in court over what happens to the fossil fuels when they arrive at the end of the pipeline. Concerns over climate change, water safety, and air quality could shut down new pipeline projects.

COMPANY RESPONSIBILITY

Energy companies such as Chevron, working in the Permian Basin, are trying to source water from nondrinkable sources. They also consult with experts to avoid sensitive areas like **archaeological** sites and the habitats of threatened or endangered animals. They provide the highest-paying jobs in areas with a lot of poor and unemployed residents. However, environment groups aren't convinced that it is possible to both produce oil and gas and protect land and water.

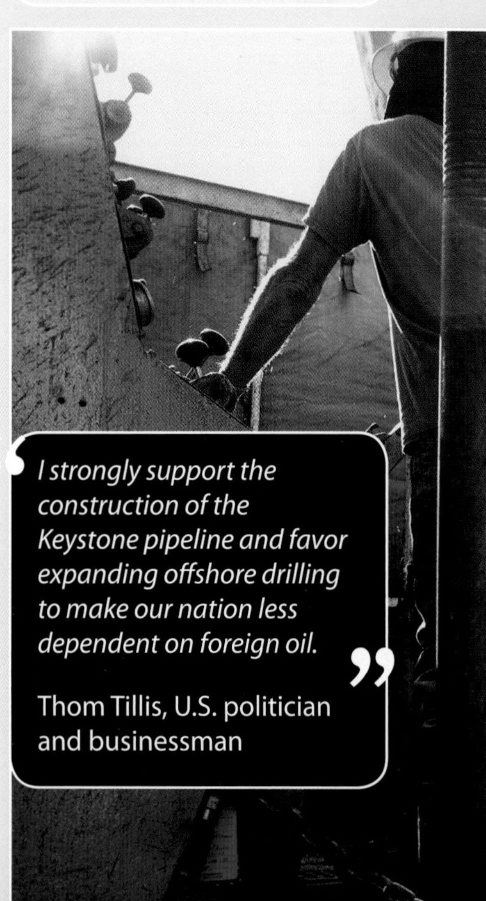

> *"I strongly support the construction of the Keystone pipeline and favor expanding offshore drilling to make our nation less dependent on foreign oil."*
>
> Thom Tillis, U.S. politician and businessman

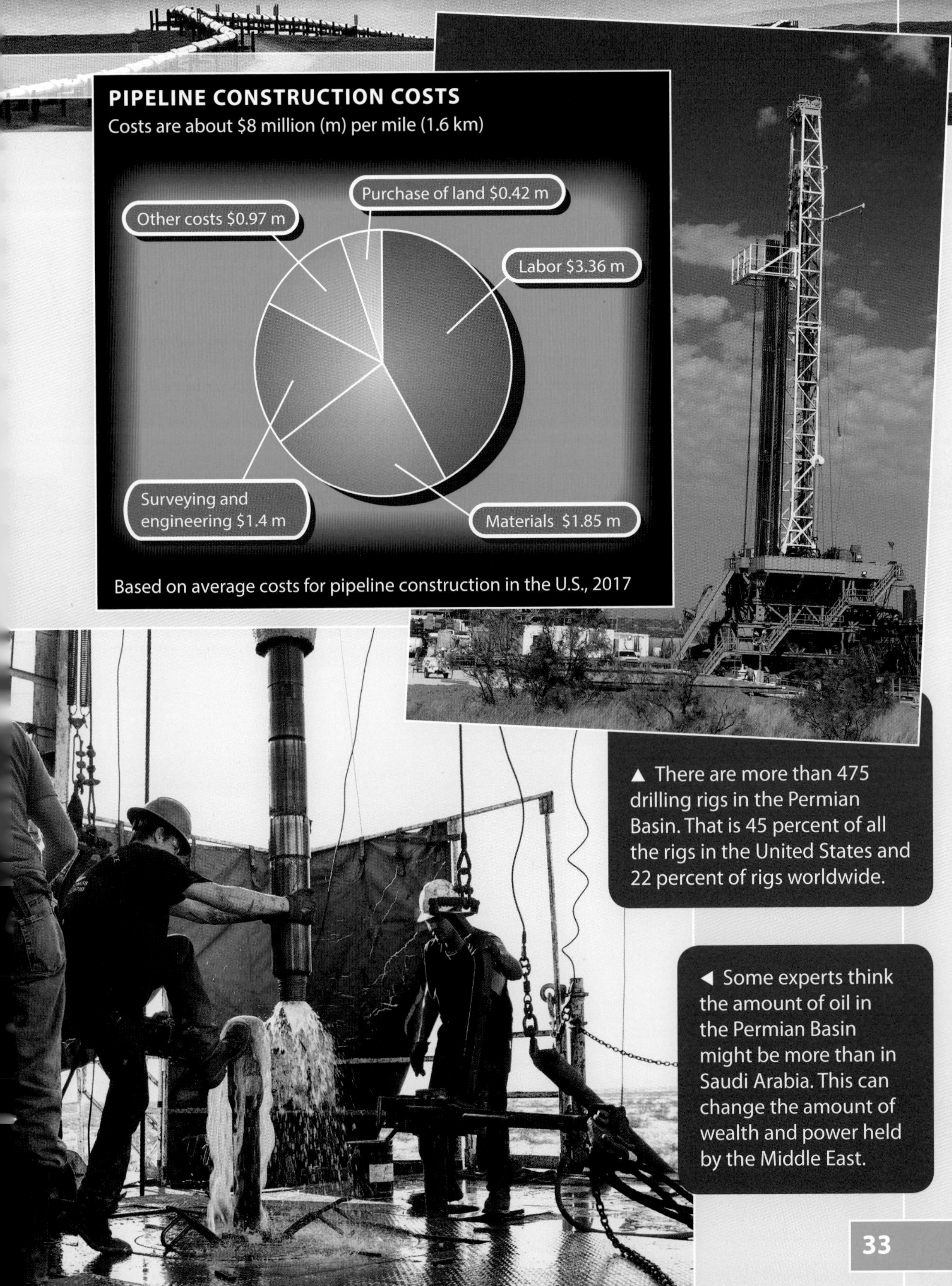

▲ There are more than 475 drilling rigs in the Permian Basin. That is 45 percent of all the rigs in the United States and 22 percent of rigs worldwide.

◀ Some experts think the amount of oil in the Permian Basin might be more than in Saudi Arabia. This can change the amount of wealth and power held by the Middle East.

FBI
INVESTIGATES ANY DESTRUCTION
OR
ATTEMPTED DESTRUCTION OF THE
TRANS ALASKA PIPELINE
OR
RELATED FACILITIES
The Hazardous Liquids Pipeline Safety Act of 1979 (Section 208(C)(2))
DEPARTMENT OF JUSTICE
FEDERAL BUREAU OF INVESTIGATION
VIOLATION PUNISHABLE BY A MAXIMUM PENALTY OF 15 YEARS IMPRISON-MENT AND OR A FINE OF $25,000
NOTIFY THE FBI IMMEDIATELY OF ANY VIOLATIONS
FEDERAL BUREAU OF INVESTIGATION
UNITED STATES DEPARTMENT OF JUSTICE
GATX 223123

▲ A small number of pipeline failures are due to vandalism. While it is rare, the FBI takes it very seriously and will investigate any intentional damage.

SEARCH TIPS

There are search tools for finding an expert on a certain topic. Type the subject into the search bar. This will help you find experts doing up-to-date research and debunk some pipeline myths.

Google Scholar: https://scholar.google.ca

Microsoft Academic: https://academic.microsoft.com

Expertise Finder: http://expertisefinder.com

PIPELINE MYTHS DEBUNKED

Some ideas on a topic can be spread over and over again until they are accepted as true without being checked. Ideas not based on facts are called myths. It is important to check all information, even if you hear that "everyone says so." Check where the information is coming from before you pass it along. Some common myths about oil and gas pipelines are:

▼ Unlike pipelines, no environmental study needs to be done when shipping oil and gas by rail across Canada. Politicians want identical safety regulations introduced.

Pipelines are unsafe

The Fraser Institute did a study comparing oil and gas transported by railroads and pipelines. While both were quite safe, pipelines had fewer spills and leaks. Rail transport has up to five times as many occurrences. The study also showed that 80 percent of pipeline leaks and spills happened in **facilities**, not in the actual line pipes. From 2003 to 2013, 99 percent of these occurrences didn't harm the environment at all.

Federal laws protect people living near pipelines

In the United States, the oil and gas industry does not have to follow many of the federal environmental laws such as the Clean Air Act, the Clean Water Act, and the Safe Drinking Water Act. In Canada, pipelines are regulated by the Pipeline Act of 1949. Landowners have to get permission for activities on their land such as fencing, plowing, or leveling the ground.

Abandoned pipelines are a risk to everyone

Pipelines must be looked after for their lifetime. In the United States, state laws vary concerning pipeline abandonment. In Canada, if a company wants to abandon a pipeline, it has to apply to the National Energy Board, a government agency that oversees the energy industry. It has to have a plan on how to remove the pipeline or clean and treat it to leave it in the ground. Once abandoned, it can never be used to carry oil and gas again.

> *"A century ago, petroleum—what we call oil—was just an obscure commodity; today it is almost as vital to human existence as water."*
>
> James Buchan, historian

New technology is changing the way pipelines are built and maintained. Environmental concerns have made the industry work harder to detect leaks and prevent spills. Finding ways to produce oil and gas while lowering or eliminating **carbon emissions** is the goal for many companies.

One of the major causes of climate change is the rising level of carbon dioxide in our atmosphere. The latest equipment to monitor pipelines includes infrared cameras, sound sensors, and wireless monitors. The goal is to prevent leaks and spills, but also to find and fix them as quickly as possible if they do happen.

REDUCING EMISSIONS

Cenovus is a Canadian **oil sands** producer. Its goal is to eventually have zero-emissions oil. That means getting oil out of the ground and to its destination without raising the level of pollution or causing any climate change. Right now they plan to decrease their emissions by one-third by 2026.

LOW RISK HIGH RISK

WHAT'S AT STAKE?

With world use of oil and gas products rising, how important is it for the oil and gas industry to cut emissions of methane and carbon dioxide?

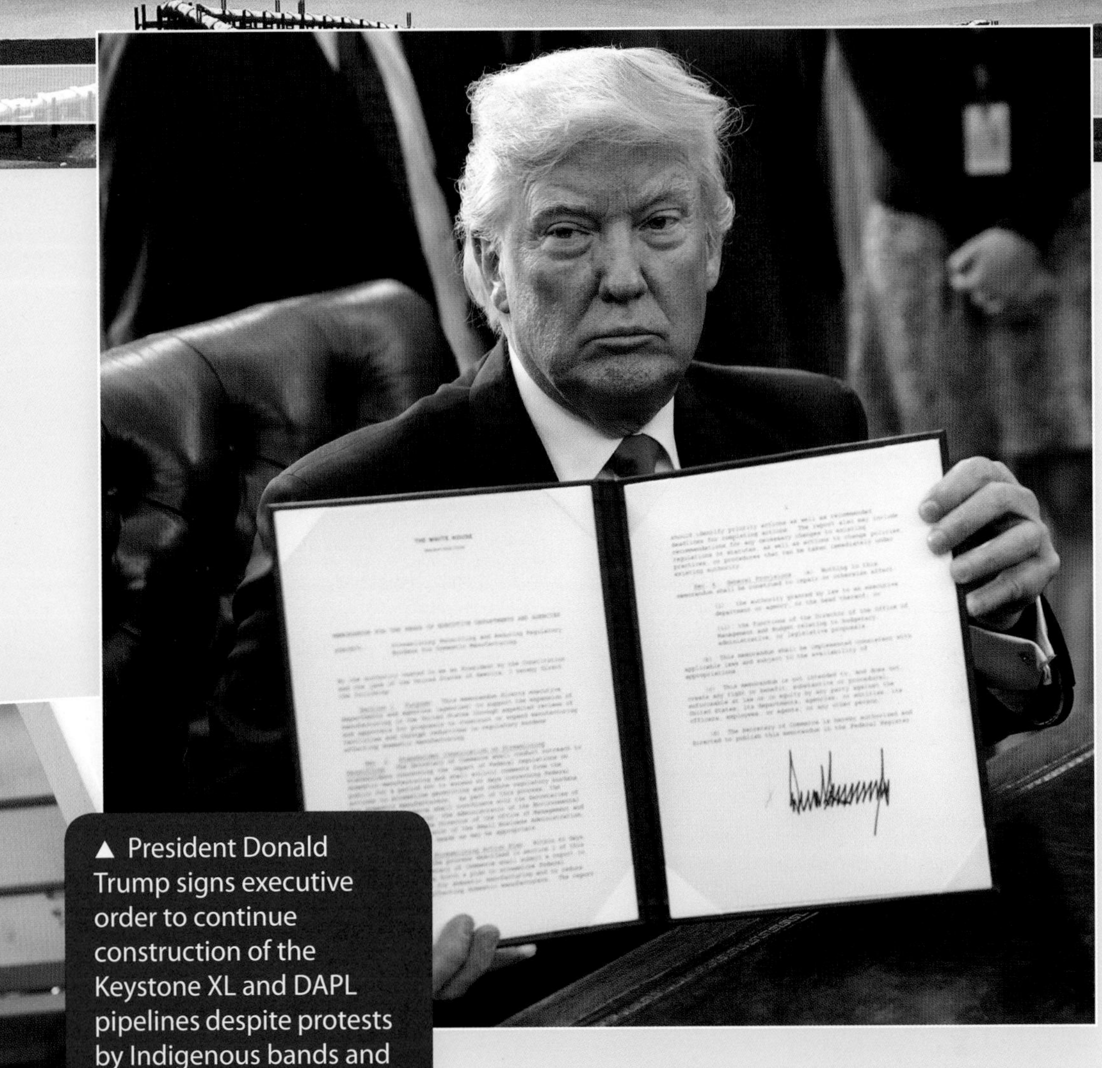

▲ President Donald Trump signs executive order to continue construction of the Keystone XL and DAPL pipelines despite protests by Indigenous bands and environmental groups.

◀ A Cenovus oil-drilling rig in Alberta, Canada. Cenovus does more than 2 billion dollars worth of business with First Nations and Métis-owned companies in northern Alberta. Up to 40 percent of the community's budget is business activity with Cenovus.

Along the same lines are companies trying to achieve **zero carbon** natural gas. A new system has been developed that captures all carbon dioxide about to be released into the atmosphere. One of these natural gas power plants was opened in Texas in 2016 by NET Power. There are plans to build another larger plant in the future.

But how effective are these programs? Statistics from both the United States and Canada show that **greenhouse emissions** from oil and gas use are rising. We are using more oil and gas for transportation, heating, and daily use than ever before. While many companies are committed to reducing emissions, the progress is slow.

Oil and gas pipelines crisscross every continent on Earth except Antarctica. After the United States, the largest users of oil and oil products are China, India, and Japan. For natural gas, the United States is again the biggest user, followed by Russia, China, and Iran. The rate of oil and gas being used is rising. Countries like China, Japan, and India don't have their own oil sources. They **import** crude oil by pipeline from other countries such as Saudi Arabia.

POWER AND POLITICS

Pipelines are vital for countries like Germany and Italy that import most or all of their fuel. Russia and Saudi Arabia both have huge oil **reserves**. Building pipelines into Europe brings money and power to these countries. When Russia and Ukraine had a conflict over gas prices and supplies, Russia shut off all gas to Ukraine. The conflict was resolved but Ukraine is looking to find suppliers of its energy needs in other countries.

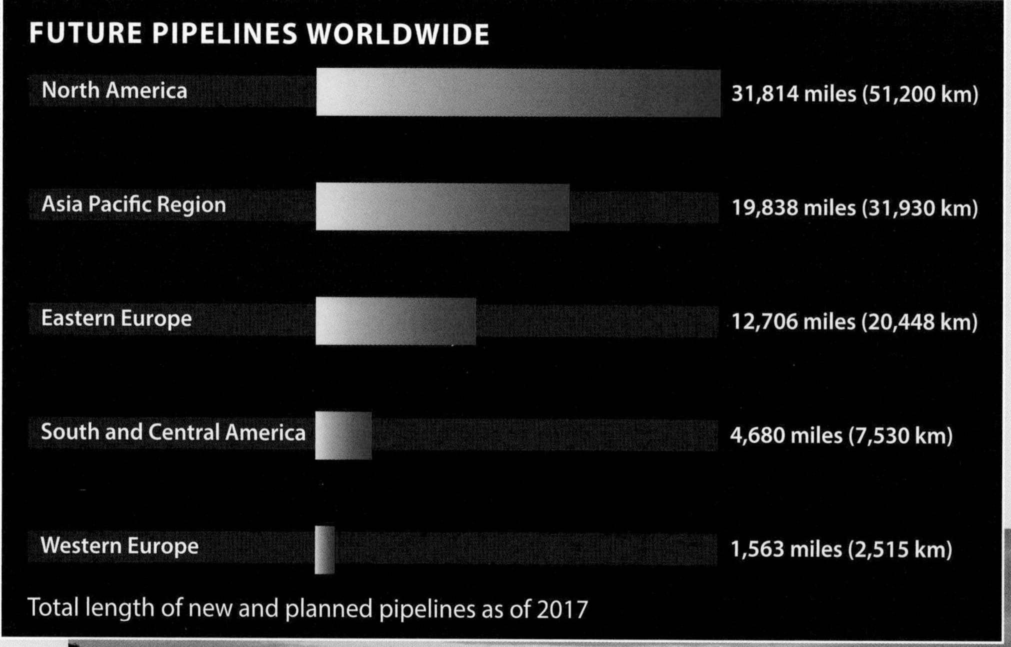

ABORIGINAL CONCERNS

Australia is dealing with its own version of the Standing Rock conflict. The Northern Gas Pipeline (NGP) is an underground pipeline that would connect the gas fields in the north part of the country with gas markets in the east. But that pipeline would cross Aboriginal lands. The traditional owners of the land, the Wakaya, are upset about damage to the environment and their sacred sites. A new pipeline, the Western Slopes Pipeline, has met so much resistance that it might not go ahead. Farmers, whose land would be crossed, blocked access and insisted it would ruin their livelihood and communities.

> *"Russia is further expanding its massive natural gas pipelines network for exports. The country is building pipelines to transport natural gas from its production centers to demand centers such as China, Japan, India and Europe."*
>
> Soorya Tejomoortula, oil and gas analyst at GlobalData

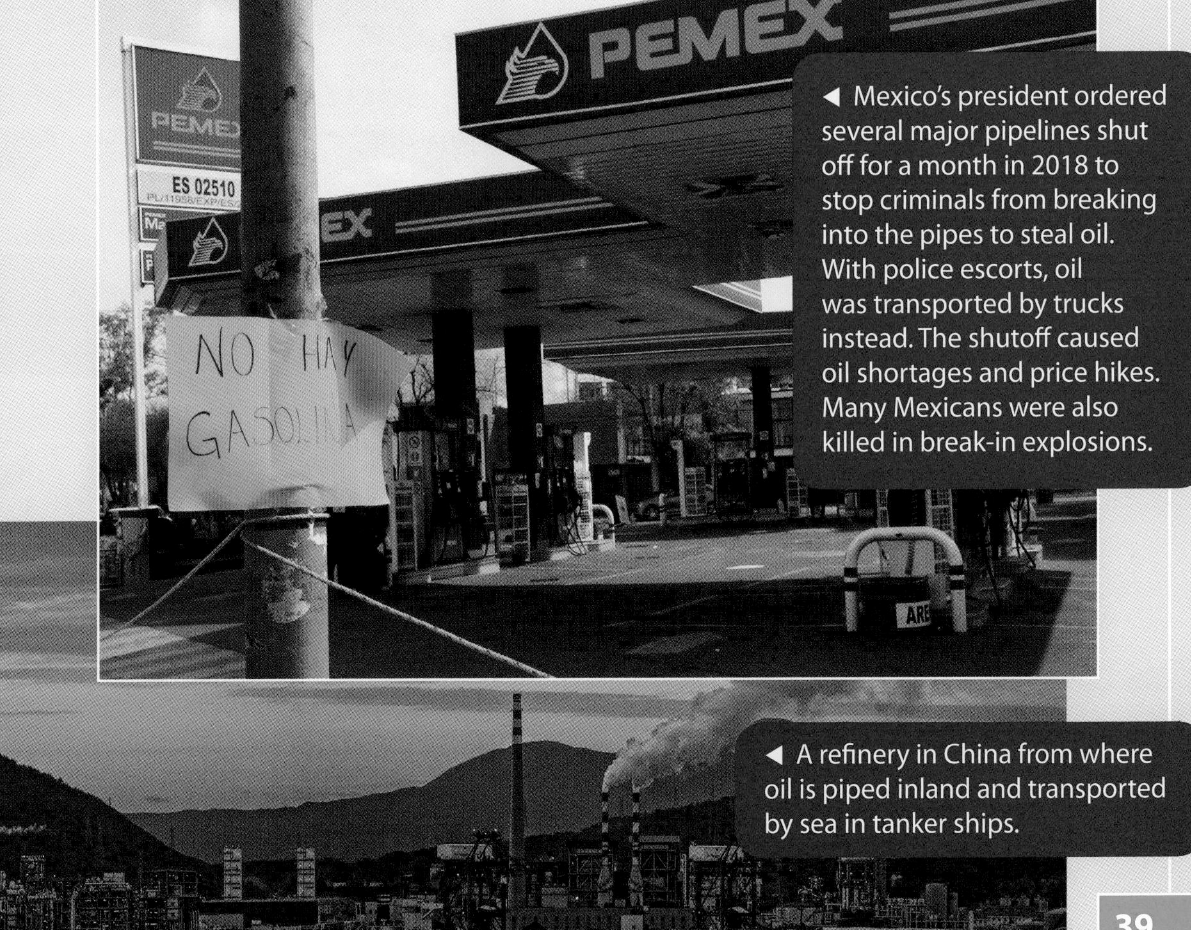

◄ Mexico's president ordered several major pipelines shut off for a month in 2018 to stop criminals from breaking into the pipes to steal oil. With police escorts, oil was transported by trucks instead. The shutoff caused oil shortages and price hikes. Many Mexicans were also killed in break-in explosions.

◄ A refinery in China from where oil is piped inland and transported by sea in tanker ships.

6 GET INVOLVED

Now that you have researched the history, background, and current state of your topic, what next? With an issue that is ongoing, you need to stay informed. It's important to keep up to date because as new events happen or new studies are finished, the situation and our understanding of it changes. For the oil and gas pipeline topic, some of the changing **factors** include new projects, new technology, planned protests, and more plant and animal species on the threatened and endangered lists.

▲ Residents vote on whether or not to allow a pipeline near their community. They cannot make an informed decision on the risks and benefits without getting all the facts.

SEARCH TIPS

When looking at websites, address extensions can help pinpoint what sort of information you may be getting.

.gov (government)—restricted to use by government entities.

.org (organization)—anyone can register for this, although it is often used for nonprofit organizations and charities.

.com (commercial)—originally for businesses, it is the most widely used extension.

Country extensions:

.ca Canada
.au Australia
.uk United Kingdom
.ru Russia
.de Germany

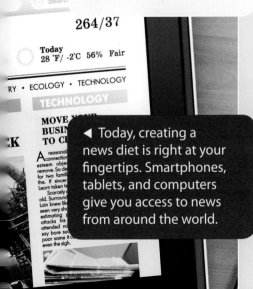

CHECK AND RECHECK

Try to keep a balanced view at all times. Getting your news on the issue of pipelines from only the oil and gas industry or from only environmental groups will not give you the whole picture. It is also important to use different media for your **news diet**. Newspapers, magazines, documentaries, reports, and statistics all give different types of information.

A vital step in gathering news is to verify your sources. Ask yourself if the reports were written by experts on the subject. Are statistics, charts, and graphs backed up with scientific research? Use primary **evidence** whenever you can, and remember the Time and Place Rule. It is also important to check who has written an article or created a website. Is the person or group objective or do they have a viewpoint they want others to agree with? Is an organization trying to sell you something? These are red flags when you are gathering your sources.

ASK QUESTIONS, CHALLENGE FACTS

Even trustworthy sources can accidentally pass on misinformation. Fact-checking is a skill that will help you all through your life. Look to see where data comes from. Look up the study or census records to fact-check. Ask questions if something doesn't make sense to you. Scientists or experts are usually happy to answer questions as long as you are respectful of their time and keep your requests short and clear. Challenging information and ideas will help you become a critical thinker.

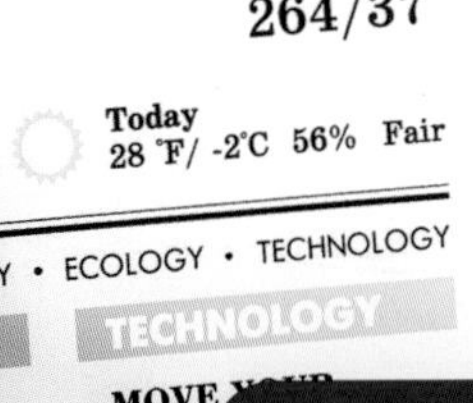

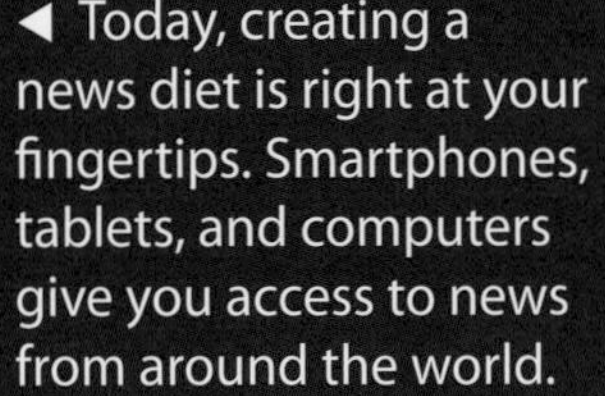

◄ Today, creating a news diet is right at your fingertips. Smartphones, tablets, and computers give you access to news from around the world.

THINKING AND ACTING FOR YOURSELF

Everyone would like to make their community, country, and planet a better place to live. But figuring out how you can play a part in that isn't always easy. Use sources such as these to stay informed about the oil and gas pipelines debate:

- fact-based news media on the Internet such as the Cable News Network (CNN) and National Public Radio (NPR)
- major newspapers and magazines such as *Time, The New York Times, The Wall Street Journal,* and *USA Today*
- TV documentaries about the topic
- radio interviews, panels, and discussions with workers, employers, business leaders, and politicians about pipeline issues
- Google Alerts for news stories about pipeline incidents
- websites of the United States Department of Energy and Canada's National Energy Board and Natural Resources Canada.

Seeing all sides of an issue helps you form an opinion that will allow you to act with clear goals in mind. Will you join a protest to bring attention to the environmental dangers of oil and gas pipelines? Will you change the products and types of energy you use in your daily life to decrease the demand for oil and gas? Maybe you will decide that a career in developing renewable energy is something to strive for.

Having a reliable source of fuel for your home or vehicle is desirable. But having a healthy, sustainable planet is equally important. Finding a solution that addresses both sides of this oil and gas pipeline issue is not an easy task, but you will make a good start by getting informed and staying informed.

SEARCH TIPS

In search windows on the Internet:

• Use quotation marks around a phrase to search for that exact combination of words (for example, "oil and gas pipelines").

• Use the minus sign to eliminate certain words from your search (for instance, pipelines–jet fuel).

• Use a colon and an extension to search a specific site (for example, Trans Mountain:.gov for all government website mentions of the pipeline).

• Use the word Define and a colon to search for word definitions (such as Define: fracking).

▶ The Global Day of Action march against climate change took place in Toronto in April 2017. Addressing the damage caused by fossil fuels is one step in protecting Earth.

▶ From inventing new energy sources to making their voices heard in communities and in government, informed youth are leading the way in demanding changes to help protect the planet.

GLOSSARY

action group A group that tries to bring about change usually by discussion, and sometimes by force

agendas Underlying plans or proposals

analyzing Studying in detail, thoroughly

archaeological Having to do with the study of historic or prehistoric people and culture

biofuels Fuel created from living matter

bottleneck Blockage

carbon emissions Carbon dioxide released by the burning of fossil fuels

community Collection of people who live in an area

compensation Money given to make up for loss or injury

contaminated Polluted

controversy Disagreement

crude oil Oil from the ground that has not been refined or processed

databases Organized collections of information

debate Discussion where all sides and perspectives of a topic are considered

dependable Reliable

dependence Relying on something

discrimination Unjust treatment or behavior against a group of people

economy The wealth and resources of a country

ecosystems Communities of living things

evidence Information or facts that prove if something is true

facilities Buildings or structures used for a specific purpose

factors The parts that contribute to a result

fault lines Large breaks in Earth's surface where earthquakes take place

First Nations In Canada, the Indigenous peoples below the Arctic Circle

fossil fuels Fuels formed from the remains of living organisms long ago, especially crude oil and natural gas

fossil record The remains or imprint of organisms left in rock that tell Earth's history of life

fracking Injecting pressurized liquid into underground rocks to release oil and gas

greenhouse emissions Gases in the atmosphere that hold in heat

heavy metals Dense metals that can be poisonous

impact Have a strong effect on something

import Bring goods in from another country

incidents Problematic events

Indigenous peoples Original inhabitants of a region or country; sometimes called First Nations, Aboriginal, or Native people

interpretations Explanations of the meaning of something

key Main, most important

land claims Legal statements by Indigenous groups of their desire to reclaim territory

lobby Try to influence laws and decisions of politicians

manufacturing Making something using machinery

marine Found in the sea

media Mass communications such as radio, TV, books, and the Internet

news diet Sources of information for daily events

objective Not taking sides

oil sands Sandstone or sand containing oil

opposing On a different side

perspectives Viewpoints

petrochemical A chemical created from oil and natural gas

petroleum products Materials made from crude oil

politicians Citizens' representatives that serve in government

pressurized Under great force

refineries Where crude oil is processed into other products

renewable energies Energy sources that do not run out such as solar or wind power

reserves Supplies of a product such as stored amounts of oil and gas

social media Websites and computer software that let people communicate and share information

society People living and working together in an organized way

specialized Detailed knowledge on one subject

statistics A type of math that deals with the collection, analysis, and presentation of numerical data; also the numerical data itself

toxic Poisonous or harmful

toxins Poisons

treaties Contracts or agreements, usually over land or resources

wetlands Land full of water, such as marshes

zero carbon Causing no overall release of carbon dioxide into the atmosphere

SOURCE NOTES

QUOTATIONS

p. 5: https://bit.ly/2z4YSUf
p. 11: https://www.sierraclub.org/press-releases/2018/10/breaking-mountain-valley-pipeline-loses-authority-cross-streams-and-wetlands
p. 17: https://trib.in/2DFlKgK
p. 21: https://www.nrdc.org/sites/default/files/glo_09111001a.pdf
p. 23: https://bit.ly/2K4O2BW
p. 24: https://www.bbc.com/news/world-us-canada-38214346
p. 29: https://bit.ly/2zXM8Qs
p. 32: https://bit.ly/2z7PaAs
p. 35: https://www.newstatesman.com/node/164761
p. 39: https://bit.ly/2KpFybd

REFERENCES USED FOR THIS BOOK

Chapter 1: Pipelines Controversy, pp. 4–7
https://www.aboutpipelines.com/en/pipeline-101/whats-in-the-pipelines/
https://bit.ly/2OKntT6
https://www.canada.ca/en/national-energy-board.html

Chapter 2: How to Get Informed, pp. 8–13
https://bit.ly/2Fni45h
https://globalnews.ca/tag/pipeline/
http://researchguides.njit.edu/evaluate/bias
https://westernreservepublicmedia.org/history/analyze.htm
https://www.timeforkids.com
https://www.tweentribune.com

Chapter 3: How Did We Get Here?, pp. 14–19
https://www.aboutpipelines.com/en/pipeline-101/pipeline-history/
https://tgam.ca/2DmM4vl
http://pipeline101.org/are-pipelines-safe
https://www.nrcan.gc.ca/energy-facts
https://www.canadasnaturalgas.ca/en
https://www.eia.gov/
https://www.energy.gov/

Chapter 4: Information Literacy, pp. 20–29
https://bit.ly/2za1nVs
https://www.eenews.net/stories/1060007532
https://bit.ly/2zXM8Qs
https://www.thoughtco.com/environmental-consequences-of-oil-spills-1204088
https://standwithstandingrock.net
https://www.nationalgeographic.com/environment/global-warming/biofuel/

Chapter 5: Recent Developments, pp. 30–39
https://bit.ly/2vtc5qC
https://www.chevron.com/projects/permian
https://www.statista.com/topics/3185/us-greenhouse-gas-emissions/
https://prn.to/2DEres9
https://bit.ly/2zbvY4W
https://globalnews.ca/news/4064038/crude-by-rail-shipments-double-energy-pipelines/
https://bit.ly/2Fmr9uV
https://cepa.com/en/
https://www.capp.ca/canadian-oil-and-natural-gas
https://www.worldoil.com/topics/production
https://www.kindermorgan.com/

Chapter 6: Get Involved, pp. 40–43
https://www.realsimple.com/work-life/technology/fact-check-internet
https://nyti.ms/2zG8OlX

FIND OUT MORE

Finding good source material on the Internet can sometimes be a challenge. When analyzing how reliable the information is, consider these points:

- Who is the author of the page? Is it an expert in the field or a person who experienced the event?

- Is the site well known and up to date? A page that has not been updated for several years probably has out-of-date information.

- Can you verify the facts with another site? Always double-check information.

- Have you checked all possible sites? Don't just look on the first page a search engine provides.

- Remember to try government sites and research papers.

- Have you recorded website addresses and names? Keep this data for a later time so you can backtrack and verify the information you want to use.

WEBSITES

Learn about oil and other fossil fuels.
https://climatekids.nasa.gov/fossil-fuels-oil/

Where does oil come from?
http://www.kids.esdb.bg/oil.html

How do we get natural gas?
http://www.kids.esdb.bg/naturalgas.html

Find out how to become an Earth Ranger.
http://www.earthrangers.org/about/

BOOKS

Bang, Molly. *Buried Sunlight: How Fossil Fuels Have Changed the Earth.* Blue Sky Press, 2014.

Bright, Michael. *From Oil Rig to Gas Pump.* Crabtree Publishing, 2016.

Drummond, Allan. *Energy Island.* Square Fish, 2015.

Olson, Elsie. *Natural Gas Energy.* ABDO Publishing, 2018.

Paleja, Shaker. *Power Up!* Annick Press, 2015.

ABOUT THE AUTHOR

Natalie Hyde has written more than 75 fiction and nonfiction books for kids. She shares her home with a little leopard gecko and a cat that desperately wants to eat it.

INDEX